DAD'S

CHILD SUPPORT

ACTION PLAN

DAD'S
CHILD SUPPORT
ACTION PLAN

INSIDER SECRETS TO WINNING
IN CHILD SUPPORT COURT

DAVID T. PISARRA, ESQ.

LIBERO MEDIA

DAD's CHILD SUPPORT ACTION PLAN
Copyright © 2025 by DAVID PISARRA, ESQ.
Published by Libero Media an imprint of
American Ghost Media

ISBN: 979-8-9924096-2-8 (Paperback)
ISBN: 979-8-9924096-3-5 (Ebook)

LEGAL DISCLAIMER

Hi Dad. I want to let you know that buying this book, or reading this book, is not setting up an attorney client relationship. You are NOT hiring me as your lawyer here.

I'm NOT going to be representing you in family court.

What we are going to be doing is giving you education and tools so that you can represent yourself when you go into family court or child support court. This is the standard legal disclaimer of, I'm not responsible for anything that happens to you as a result of going to family court.

I do want you to remember that you're awesome, and I think that you have a great opportunity to go spend more time with your kids and keep your child support at the minimum of what it should be.

HEY DAD!

**Are You Ready to Be a Badass in Family Court?
Join Dad's Law School VIP Program!**

You're a **Vitally Important Parent (VIP).**

Learn How to Prove It To The Judge!

**As a Member, You Get Everything You Need
to Show Up Strong in Court:**

- **CHILD CUSTODY ACTION PLAN**

- **EVIDENCE & DISCOVERY Video Course**

- **WEEKLY Live Group Coaching Sessions**

- **Court-Ready Sample Documents
and MORE!**

SCAN TO JOIN TODAY!

A father's job is to be the safe place from which his children dare the world.

SCAN THE QR CODE FOR YOUR <u>FREE</u> AUDIOBOOK READ BY THE AUTHOR!

HEY DAD!

Thanks for picking up this book. I hope it helps you.

I know not everyone wants to just read a book, some people like to listen to it as well. That's why I created the audio book version, that is all yours for FREE! to get your audiobook download just scan the below QR code.

Thanks for being a Great Dad, and remember that I think you're F'n Awesome!

~David

TABLE OF CONTENTS

DEDICATION

I'm dedicating this book to the fathers who are doing all that they can to be in their children's lives. To the ones who work one, two or three jobs to provide for their families. To the dads who make unrecognized sacrifices so their children can have a better life. To the dads who are rocking 2 year old boots so their kids have new Jordans.

This book is dedicated to the dads who want the best for their children - no matter what.

*The best inheritance a father leaves
is the memory of his presence.*

FOREWORD

For the past 27-ish years I've represented fathers in court. These are men who are fighting to be part of their child's life. In all that time I've had just two dads who didn't want to be a part of their child's life. Two dads out of hundreds of men.

The first was a man who had a true "one night stand" and ended up with twins. His life was set up to be a bachelor, he made no promises of lifelong love and support to anyone but himself. He was all business. He wanted to be a "lone wolf".

True to his word he showed up at the child support hearing, paid what he had to, and then moved to some resort town in Central America - never to be seen or heard from again.

The second one was a douchebag. He got mom pregnant and when it came to the DNA testing, he sent in his brother. That didn't work by the way. I don't recommend it.

The other men that I've represented over the years have been fighting for more time, more access and more connection with their children. Most of the dads recognize they have a responsibility to support their children and do so without complaining. They accept that they will pay support - what they don't accept and what they resent, is how hard it is to have time with their children.

I've had many a father say they'd pay more if their ex would allow them to have more time. I've had many fathers who have the children dropped off by mom when she wants to leave and go enjoy life with her new boyfriend, and the dad won't go back to court to recalculate the child support because he knows she'll take the kids back if he takes away "her money".

I've had fathers who were awarded custody, and the mom was ordered to pay child support. And she won't pay. Many of these dad refused to go after her for the support saying, "I don't need her money, and it's too much trouble."

There is a brutal double standard when it comes to child support. Dads often will prioritize the children over the support if mom is supposed to pay it. Moms will prioritize money, over the children when dads are supposed to pay it.

I know dads who are working 12 and 14 hour and 16 hour days, only to be told they are "deadbeats".

They're not.

They're fucking heroes who should be honored and respected; not demeaned and insulted.

These dads are heroes who are court ordered to pay support. They work to earn the money for the support, then they are blamed for not being around for their kids while mom prevents them from seeing the kids. It's a set-up to fail. No man should have that happen to them.

This book is to help those Dads get respect from a court system that doesn't value their contributions. It's to help Dads regain their self-respect and to understand that they are fighting a battle against a ruthless, relentless enemy - a system that rewards victimhood.

David Pisarra, Esq.

Time spent is the only currency that matters to a child counting their father's wealth.

> *"We never know the love of a parent until we become parents ourselves."*
>
> —Henry Ward Beecher

INTRODUCTION

Hey Dad, this book is written to explain to you the basics of child support. The goal is to give you an understanding of what the history of child support is, why it's important today, and what you can do to minimize your child support obligations and maximize your child support activities. And the reason why I say that, is money is one thing, but the reality is, child support should not be just money.

Child support should also be time with your kid, teaching them, helping them with schoolwork, teaching them new skills. Child support is not just money. Most people think of it as only a money issue, because that's what the state and the court is concerned with. That's what, frankly, mom's concerned with.

The reality is, you need to be looking at it from both a money perspective, and also a time perspective. Time with your kids is the most precious thing and it's the ONE THING that you can never get back.

You can always make more money. You're a man. You know how to do this. The issue is getting the maximum amount of time with your kids so that you can give them the most emotional, physical and educational support that they need.

The finest fathers are made, not in moments of triumph, but in moments of showing up.

THE QUICK START GUIDE

This Quick Start Guide will help you in preparing your case to modify your Child Support.

REMEMBER, when you go to court you have to have EVERYTHING READY THAT DAY. The Most Common Mistake I see people make in court is to tell a Judge, "I have the evidence at home, I can bring it."

DON'T DO THAT. DON'T BE THAT GUY!

When you have a court date, THAT'S THE DAY. YOU HAVE TO HAVE IT WITH YOU, GIVE A COPY TO THE OTHER SIDE **BEFORE THE HEARING.** :

Here's the short version of what you need to get started BEFORE you file with the court for a change of support.

1. Get a copy of the most recent Court Order. – Go to the courthouse and find the Clerk's Office or the Child Support Office and ask for a copy of the most recent court order in your case.

2. Make a list of all the payments you've made to make sure they are all credited. – Use a spreadsheet like Excel or Google Sheets to prepare a list of all your payments, and have the proof with you. The bank statements that show your check cleared, the money order receipts, the Zelle or PayPal or CashApp transfers. You can only get credit for what you can prove.

3. Create your Dad's Diary to show you've been seeing your child and when. – This is a crucial piece of your case, to show you're an engaged dad, or that you keep trying to see the child and Mom wont let you.

4. What do you know about Mom's work and income? - Her income counts and is used to figure out the child support you pay. Make sure there's a number for her income, even if it's just minimum wage for 40 hours a week it can help.

5. What do you know about where she works? – When you know where she works you can ask for her paystubs to know what she's making. Keep her honest. You can get a subpoena issued by the Court Clerk if you need to find out her income. Your local court can help you with issuing a subpoena. [More about how to do that in the Discovery Course at DadsLawSchool.com]

6. Does she have PayPal? Venmo? CashApp? - Maybe get a copy of those records with a subpoena. You can get a subpoena issued by the Court Clerk if you need to find out her income. Your local court can help you with issuing a subpoena. [More about how to do that in the Discovery Course at DadsLawSchool.com]

7. Is your child 'special needs'? if mom is getting money for the government for taking care of the child under the "In Home Care Services" program, you should make that you know how much and that it's included as her income, because if it's her full-time job, that's her income.

FOUR STEPS TO CRUSHING IT IN CHILD SUPPORT COURT: A BASIC GUIDE

This easy-to-follow guide will help you handle child support court with confidence. You'll learn how to gather your evidence, file and deliver your paperwork the right way, find information about the other parent's income, and get ready for your court date. By following these four simple steps, you'll be better prepared and have a stronger chance of a good result in court.

STEP ONE: Get Your Evidence Ready

This initial step is crucial for building a strong foundation for your case. Gather all necessary documents to accurately represent your financial situation and the current child support arrangement.

- **Your Income:** Collect your last two months' pay stubs or documentation of income from your business. This provides the court with a clear picture of your current earnings.

- **Payment History:** List all payments made to the mother or the State Disbursement Unit. This demonstrates your compliance with existing orders and helps track any discrepancies.

- **Current Court Order:** Obtain a copy of the current child support order. This serves as the baseline for any modifications you are seeking.

- **Tax Returns:** Have your last two years' tax returns readily available. These provide a comprehensive overview of your income and financial history.

- **Prepare the Forms:** Complete the necessary forms, specifically the California FL-300 Request for Order and FL-150 Income and Expense Declaration (or their equivalents in your state). These forms are essential for formally requesting a modification or adjustment to the child support order.

STEP TWO: File and Serve the Request for Order

Properly filing and serving the Request for Order is essential for ensuring the court has jurisdiction and that all parties are notified.

- **File with the Court Clerk:** Take the completed forms to the Court Clerk, along with three copies: one for the court, one for your records, and one to serve on your ex.

- **Serve the Papers:** Have the court-stamped papers served on your ex. Any adult other than you can serve the papers and then complete the Proof of Service. If the Child Support Agency is enforcing the collection of support, they also need to be given a copy of the papers.

- **File Proof of Service:** File the Proof of Service on your ex (and the Child Support Agency, if necessary) with the court. This confirms that the other party has been officially notified of the proceedings.

STEP THREE: Get Her Money Information

Understanding the other parent's financial situation is just as important as knowing your own. This information helps the court make a fair and accurate determination of child support obligations.

- **Her Income:** Obtain her last two months' pay stubs or documentation of income from her business. This provides insight into her current earnings.

- **Bank Statements:** If you know where she banks, try to get her bank statements for the past year. The Court Clerk can issue a Subpoena to help you with this if necessary. This can reveal additional income sources or financial resources.

STEP FOUR: Prepare for Court

Thorough preparation is key to presenting your case effectively and achieving the best possible outcome.

- **Child Support Calculator:** Go to the Child Support Website for your state and get an "Estimated Child Support" amount based on the information you've gathered. This gives you an idea of what the court might order based on both parents' incomes and other relevant factors.

- **Prepare Talking Points:** Prepare bullet points of what you want to say to the judge. Organize your thoughts and focus on the key issues you want to address. This will help you stay on track and present your case clearly and concisely.

The father who admits his mistakes raises children who forgive their own.

"What makes you a man is not the ability to have a child—it's the courage to raise one."

—Barack Obama

HISTORY OF CHILD SUPPORT

Here's a short history of child support, because it's important for you to understand that the way things are today, is not the way they've always been. Historically, prior to the early 1970s, child custody was granted to the parent who had the job, because the courts thought, 'that's the parent that can support the child'.

What this meant was men and women would get married, have children, and upon a divorce, the kids would go with dad.

That's why, in the 1970s there was a big feminist movement to change to no-fault divorce, which made it easier for women to divorce their husbands. The court applied what's called the tender years doctrine. The goal was to take children who were in those very, very first years of their life and put them with the parent that was, in theory, the most nurturing, the one that had the most ability to emotionally care for the child. Historically, that was a big shift, because we used to have the concern that the child had to be taken care of with food, housing, clothing, and schooling.

That's why, historically, children were given to the Father upon a divorce, because he was the one that actually had the most amount of resources, because he's the one that had the job, access to credit, and most of the assets.

This is why women were not actually divorcing men, because as soon as they divorced the man, they experienced a huge drop in their net worth, their income, and as a consequence of that, they weren't able to provide for their children, and so the court would then take the kids away from them.

In the 1970s when that started shifting, when no-fault divorce came in, we started to look at how we're going to reconfigure families. What was happening was, women were divorcing men, and now the children were going with mom under the tender years doctrine, because she's the "better parent".

You need to be ready to argue to the court that you should have more time, and mom can get a job. I cover that in greater detail in the companion book and video course, DAD's Child Custody Action Plan which is available for you at www. DadsLawSchool.com.

14

The problem with that is we now had a parent who didn't have a job, didn't have access to credit, probably didn't have a whole lot of resources, and was going on public assistance. This is where welfare came into play.

A lot of public resources were being applied for by women in order to support children. Dads were not supporting their kids because there was no court order in place to support the children. As a consequence of that, moms started going to court and saying, "I need to make dad pay to support the child. Even if I'm not going to be married to him, he still has to support the kid".

That's when the child support system was changed. This was in the early 1970s and the goal primarily was to provide for the child financially, but also to keep mom and the child off of the public dole.

Moms were going to child support court and to avoid getting welfare, they would ask for child support. That's where the motivation to change the system came from. Politicians and lobbyists started doing what they do, making laws with the best of intentions that get perverted and abused.

The original goal being to provide for the child, not have the state provide for the child, but have the parents provide for the child.

What that really meant though was that DAD had to provide for the child, and mom got to continue being a stay-at-home mom who didn't have to work.

There are regulations that require both parents to support the children to the best of their abilities. This is one of those areas where it gets pretty gray.

The Dads are generally the ones who are working, and mom's generally the one who's not working as much. She may have a part time job. She may have no job. She may have been a stay-at-home mom. These are now factors that are going to impact child support.

When a couple breaks up, if the court has to decide what child custody is going to be, and what the child support is going to be, no one is going to be happy.

This is where the problem starts. Men are coming into court saying, "I've got a job. I can take care of the kid. Why can't I have 50% custody?" While Mom's saying, "No, I can't get a job. I need him to pay support so I can take care of the kid, because the kid has to go to school, needs to get to tutors, karate classes, football practice, rugby practice, whatever their lifestyle is".

This is a natural set of factors that are in conflict with each other. Dad who's concerned with having time with his kid, and mom who's got concerns about being able to make her rent. That's where we are today.

We're having a huge social change in men who are now stepping up saying, "I want more time with my kid. I should be able to provide for my child, not just financially, but also emotionally. I should be able to provide housing, have time to do homework, and have an opportunity to regularly teach them the way I operate in the world'. While moms are saying, "Well, that's not necessarily in the child's best interest, because they're going to be spending too much time in a car. You're not able, because of your work, to have the time for the child".

These are just some of the factors that a judge will look at when you go into court. You need to be able to argue why you have the opportunity and the ability to be a parent to get more time, which will naturally lower your child support because it makes it easier for mom to get a job and contribute to the child's support.

This book is focused on the financial aspects of child support, but understand that a big factor in your child support calculation is going to be how much time you spend with the child. That's where you need to make the argument to the judge that 1) you're as capable, 2) you're available, 3) you're ready to show up 4) you're ready to have more time with the kid 5) Mom needs to get a job 6) Mom needs to change her lifestyle 7) the child's old enough to go from her house to yours, and 8) that you are living close to Mom so the child will not have huge commute time in a car.

When all of that is in your favor the court should be deciding on a more equitable child support number for both time and money.

The strongest fathers carry
what cannot be seen.

"Much of life, fatherhood included, is the story of knowledge acquired too late: If only I'd known then what I know now, how much smarter, abler, stronger, I would have been."

—Ben Fountain

HOW CHILD SUPPORT IS DETERMINED

Now some information about how child support is determined. To be honest, there's really, two or three big factors that go into this.

The #1 Factor is time.

How much time you have with your child versus how much time does mom have with the child?

That's important because it's going to have a huge impact when the court starts looking at your income versus mom's income. If mom has a lot of time, but no income, and you have a lot of income, but no time, you're going to be paying the maximum amount of child support. Which is probably mom's goal, and the goal for you is to increase your amount of time with your child.

The #2 Factor is obviously YOUR INCOME.

What you are earning, how many hours you work, what you CAN earn, what you're getting as compensation for work (like rent credit for managing a building) these are all the topics the court will look at, and Mom (or her lawyer {including the one given to her by the government}) will point out to make sure you pay the maximum child support.

But there's another factor that many Dads ignore at their own cost. They don't want to play hardball with Mom since she'll take it on him and not let him see their child, but I encourage you to make sure that it's included, because sometimes it can make a big difference in what you pay, and that's Mom's income.

MOM'S INCOME

You need to make the argument that mom's income should be increasing, because mom should have, at least, a minimum wage job. She has the same responsibility to provide for her child, that you do. In the same way you should have the opportunity to care for your child, you should be asking for as much time as you can possibly get with your child. Your goal is to make sure there is as much income on mom's side, so that there's a balance between the two of you.

Because in theory, if the two of you make the same amount of money, and you have the same amount of time with the child. Child support should be almost zero.

There may be small differences each year due to the tax deduction. If she takes it one year, and then the next year you take the deduction, it may change a little, but essentially you'd be in the same place.

This is the game that moms play who are in this for the money.

There are a lot of moms out there that are not in it just for the money. There's a lot of moms out there who are working full time jobs providing for their child, and they're the ones taking the child to school on time, get to the doctors, get to the dentist, and then dad has the opportunity to work his job, and so as a consequence of that, Mom needs some help with her finances, and that's why child support balances things out.

But there's also a lot of moms out there who are in this for maximizing that child support. Those are the moms that we need to really take a look at and give you some tools to argue against. Because what she's doing is artificially lowering her income, and artificially increasing the time that she has with the child. She's going to do everything she can to prevent you from having custody so that she has the maximum amount of custody and the minimum amount of income. That way you have the minimum amount of time for custody, and the maximum amount of income to pay child support.

CHILD SUPPORT SOFTWARE

In general, there's a very long mathematical formula to figure out child support. It's so confusing that you have to use a computer to figure out support. In California we use X-Spouse. It used to be Dissomaster. And most states have an online solution where you plug in your income, mom's income, how much time you have with the children, and a few other deductions, like health insurance, medical co-pays. If you're paying for a mortgage, what's the deductible interest that factors in.

At the end of the day, the computer just spits out a number based off of your income, mom's income, your time with the child, mom's time with the child, your deductions, mom's deductions, and then it just says, this is the monthly amount to equalize the income between the two homes, and that, in theory, is the goal to equalize the living standard between the two homes.

The reason for that is so that the child is not going from the big mansion with the big pool and all of the toys, to a dinky little studio apartment and no pool and no toys, because there's going to be this difference in lifestyle, and that's one of the reasons why child support is calculated the way it is.

The formula is designed to balance out the parties' incomes and hopefully balance out the living environment for the child, so they don't feel favoritism towards one parent whose house has a pool and the toys and all the fun stuff and feeling less than, when they're with the parent that doesn't have all of that.

That's one of the motivations behind child support, to equalize the homes so that the child has the best living environment for them growing up.

EXCEPTIONALLY HIGH EARNERS

Now there are exceptions when we're talking about child support, because there are people who are on the very, very high end of income, and they are called exceptionally high earners. The super-wealthy sometimes can opt out of the child support system. Somebody who is making a lot, lot of money, people who are making millions and millions of dollars every year, they're an exceptionally high earner. So the child support guidelines, the number that the computer spits out would be astronomical. That wouldn't make any sense. There's no reason why a child needs, let's say, a quarter million dollars a month to be supported.

The court has an option when they are dealing with someone in the extremely high earner category. Let's assume Mom only needs $15,000 a month to support that child, because that's a realistically fair number for that child. The court can deviate from the calculation and base the support on what the child actually needs.

EXCEPTIONALLY LOW EARNERS

Alternatively, on the other end of the spectrum, where dads are not making anything, the dads who are unemployed or disabled or having low wages for whatever reason. They're on the end where the court's going to be able to look at and say, based on guideline, it's going to be a very, very low number, sometimes it's $2 or $3 or $10 a month of child support. This is because the court has to allow a father to have the base minimum of housing and food, but not a car, not a cell phone.

The child support system is designed to deal with the reality of where someone is. And then it also has fail-safes, because if you're literally living at the point where all you can afford is a room for you to live in and food to survive, the court can't even order child support. If you're actually that broke, there will be a zero order for the really low end of the income range.

The true reality is most people fall in the vast middle ground. Most people make too much money to have no payment of child support. When you make enough money to support yourself beyond just barely surviving, there will be some child support order made, and that's going to be a big chunk of what your income is.

If you want to estimate your support order here's what I use as a "back of the envelope sketch" - assume you have every other weekend, a Wednesday night pizza dinner, half the holidays, and a few weeks of the summer, you're looking at about 25% of your gross paycheck for one child, and 35% for 2 children. That's gross paycheck. It's the first number before taxes.

Income Range	Child Support Estimate at 25% of Gross Paycheck 1 Child	Child Support Estimate at 35% of Gross Paycheck 2 Children
$1,000 - $2,000	$250 - $500	$350 - $700
$2,000 - $4,000	$500 - 1,000	$700 - 1,400
$4,000 - $6,000	$1,000 - $1,500	$1,400 - $2,100

Child support will change based on some of the allowed deductions, the expenses you have to pay that the court accepts. Some of the most common ones are union dues, if you have a mortgage you can use the deductible interest portion (this actually increases the amount of available cash and the child support will increase as a result). The court will include the health insurance premiums if you're paying those.

DAYCARE

Remember though that daycare only counts until the child is 13, (assuming there are no special needs for the child – I'll deal with that in a separate section) after that the IRS says it's no longer needed and is not a deduction so it also doesn't apply in family court for child support.

Daycare is also split unequally in more states these days. It used to be that it was shared 50/50 between the parties, but in California and some other states, the newest trend is to split expenses like that based on the proportion of the parties income.

For example, if Dad makes $60,000 a year ($5,000 a month), and mom makes $40,000 a year ($3,750 a month) then Dad is going to pay 2/3rd of the daycare expense to Mom's 1/3rd in addition to the regular 25% estimate of child support.

If you have a young child who's going to school and they get out at noon, and they go to a daycare provider, from 12:00 to 4:30, that allows mom to have a full time job. Dad will be paying part of that daycare so the mom can have a full time job. It's a win some, lose some.

Dad wins some because Mom's got a full time job. Dad loses some because he has to pay for part of the daycare, so that Mom can have that full time job. Her working lowers his child support on the one hand, but increases it with the daycare on the other. It's a very difficult situation, because a lot of times people want to say, well, "I'll take care of the kid after school". If they have a free afternoon, and that flexibility in their job, certainly a court can order the additional time.

Many people don't have the flexibility in their work schedule to allow them to have more time with their child. If a dad is working a nine to five job or a seven to three or some schedule along those lines, it can be difficult for the court to order that he should have the child those afternoons, because he doesn't have the free time because of his job.

EXTRACURRICULARS

Some expenses like after school sports, and other activities, may be dealt with in child support. These are more discretionary for the judge to order, often the judge will look to what the parties previously agreed to, and what are the incomes of the parties. If the child has had years of "club sports", it's likely that the court will order that continue to be paid for by the parents as it is in the child's best interest, and there is a history of it happening.

If the custodial parent suddenly signs the child up for a lot of new activities that have not been paid for previously, or that the parties don't agree on, the court is less likely to order it to be paid for by the parent who disagrees with the activity. This happens when one parent is trying to make sure the child is "too busy" to see the other parent – often this is a tactic to increase the custodial parents time, and hence add to their child support award.

CO-PAYS

The other expenses that are NOT included can be healthcare costs. Traditionally the co-pays for the doctors are split equally. Things like dental bills, and braces for the child's teeth, those are additional costs that a court normally will order be paid in addition to the regular child support, as they are considered medically necessary. Those too can be split proportionately.

HEALTH INSURANCE

Most of the time, each parent is required to pay for health insurance if it's at low or no cost through their employer. So if your employer has a group plan and you're actually able to provide health insurance for your child, you're going to have to do that, and you're going to have to split the co-pays that are $10 or $25 every time you go to the pediatrician or go to the nutritionist or you go to the dentist, that's going to get split too - because it's an expense of the child, and parents have to split the expenses.

Now some states are like California, where we've changed the system, and expenses are no longer a 50/50, split. Due to new legislation that was passed and signed by the Governor (I wonder who was behind this one!) expenses are now divided by the percentage of dad's income versus mom's income.

If dad is making twice as much money as mom's making, he's going to pay $2/3^{rd}$ of those health care expenses, and mom's only going to have to pay 1/3rd of them and we're going to apply that same percentage to the daycare.

If mom's making only 1/3 of what dad's earning, dad will have to pay for 3/4ths of that daycare. Some states are like that now, and some states are still in the old system, where it was just split equal 50/50.

Here's an income table to show you what this will mean in real life:

MOM MAKES HALF OF WHAT DAD MAKES

Mom's Income	$1,000	Mom pays 1/3rd of expenses
Dad's Income	$2,000	Dad pays 2/3rds of expenses
TOTAL INCOME	$3,000	

MOM MAKES A THIRD OF WHAT DAD MAKES

Mom's Income	$1,000	Mom pays 1/4th of expenses.
Dad's Income	$3,000	Dad pays 3/4ths of expenses
TOTAL INCOME	$4,000	

THE 'SPECIAL NEEDS' SITUATION

When a child has 'Special Needs' it adds a level of difficulty to the calculation of child support depending on what the special need is. There is a broad range of what is considered special needs and how it impacts both the costs of caring for a child, and how much it demands from the parents to provide.

The term 'Special Needs' means everything from the child who has a mild form of dyslexia and they need some additional tutoring to help with reading or math, to the child with severe cerebral palsy and will require lifetime, fulltime care. Here's an incomplete list of what is considered Special Needs:

1. ADHD – Attention Deficit Hyperactivity Disorder.

2. Autism Spectrum Disorder

3. Down Syndrome

4. Vision Impairment

5. Hearing Impairment

6. Physical Impairment

7. Cystic Fibrosis

8. Spina Bifida

9. Dyslexia / Dysnomia / Dysgraphia / Dyscalculia

10. Delayed Speech Development

11. Epilepsy

12. Diabetes

13. Asthma

14. Mental Health issues

  a. Manic/Depressive Disorder

  b. Schizophrenia

  c. Substance Abuse Disorder

If your child has one of these, or some other, special need, that needs to be properly explained to the judge, and how it impacts their day to day life, and then what that does to both parents ability to work. Sometimes, there is a stay at home parent who is receiving money from the government to provide "in home care", typically the Mom, and that should be added in to her income.

The other issue is that if it is being paid out by a parent it can be and "add on" expense, that allows a parent work, and then the cost could be split between the parents.

A father's presence is the most reliable indicator of a child's future success.

*"The best way of training the young is to train
yourself at the same time; not to admonish them, but to be
seen never doing that of which you
would admonish them."*

Plato

MOM SAYS, "I CAN'T WORK."

How do you prove somebody has income when they're not working? One of the claims that some moms make is, "I can't work."

You have to ask why not? Many times the answer is a "condition" that is hard to detect. This is a very common answer: "Well, I've got fibromyalgia, and I'm disabled, and no one will hire me because I've been a stay at home mom for too long."

We need to break that statement down and look at those arguments to see what's really happening.

PHYSICAL DISABILITY

Fibromyalgia. Does that really mean that you can't work? or does that mean that you can't work as a lineman in an electric utility when you're climbing up and down telephone poles?

Does it mean you could work in an office seated at a desk? Especially if the employer gave you Americans with Disabilities Act accommodations?

To some degree, everybody's got a skill set so they can get a job. At a bare minimum, everybody could go to work somewhere, unless they're severely disabled. Severely disabled means there's some severe physical problem or some severe mental problem that prevents them from working.

I know I'm a bit of a hardass on this one, but then again I have a friend with no arms who is an international speaker who travels the world, drives his own car, and plays the drums. So I'm not a big believer in the "I can't work" victimhood game.

If someone is truly disabled they should have a diagnosis of disability, from either Social Security or their doctors. Absent having an actual diagnosis of complete disability, everybody should be able to work, to some degree. Any parent should be able to work and should be contributing to that child's support.

WORK EXPERIENCE

It's vitally important that the court examine what it really means when somebody says, "I can't work." One of the areas to be examined is, what are their skill sets? Do they have a college degree? What have they historically done? Have they always been a stay-at-home mom? Have they ever worked in a restaurant? Have they ever worked in an office? Have they ever worked retail sales?

IMPUTATION

When I'm cross-examining a mom, I may say, "Okay, Mom, you're not working. You say you can't get a job, but we know that you could go down to one of the fast food restaurants in town and apply for a job and get a job at minimum wage, and they could hire you, and you could work a 40 hour work week at minimum wage, and you could do that four weeks out of the month. Isn't that right?"

She'll deny it, she'll say they wont hire her, or she's better than that, or she can't stand that long, or any number of other BS claims. At this point I'll ask the judge to do what's called an IMPUTATION.

The court will hear her testimony, and her ability to work, and the Court SHOULD say, "Mom, you may not be working, but I'm going to assume that you could be working, and therefore I'm going to assume what you could be earning at a bare minimum. And that's called an imputation. The court is assuming her income for purposes of calculating the right child support.

The court is saying "this is what you could be earning if you would get your butt in gear and go down to the local fast food place and apply for a job, and whether that's at the grocery store or the fast food place or the local retail store, someone will pay you a minimum wage to have a job, and you could be earning money, and you have a legal obligation to support your children, and you should get that job."

This is a big tool dads have, to ask the court to impute, to assume that mom could be making a certain amount of money, and then use that number to figure out what is fair for child support. It's a very powerful tool, and I've used it with great success, because oftentimes I can get a mom to admit that, well, she used to do this, and that job used to pay $20 an hour. Okay, well that means you used to make $20 an hour times 40 hours a week is $800 a week. Times four weeks is $3,200 a month. Well, now I'm going to ask the court to impute to mom $3,200 a month income to balance out dad's income, so that now when we're looking at what the child support should be, we're going to bring dad's number down to a more reasonable number, because if mom doesn't want to work, she doesn't have to no court can make you go get a job.

We have a 13th Amendment to the United States Constitution that prevents anybody from forcing you to work, but a court can make the assumption that you have the ability to work, and that you have the ability to earn an income based on that work, and that's what it will do when you're looking to impute income to one party or the other.

Fair Warning! This works the same way for dads. Dads can get caught up on this too. Dad could have been making, let's say, $150,000 a year as a pharmaceutical salesperson, and then decides, because he doesn't want to pay his child support, that he's going to quit his job and go get a minimum wage job. You're going to have a hard argument with the judge on that one.

That's going to be a long conversation, because the judge is going to ask, "Why can't you work as a salesman anymore? You're still able to walk and talk and work, because if you're working at a fast-food restaurant, you're able to walk and talk and work. So why can you no longer work as a pharmaceutical salesperson, earning $150,000 a year?"

Unless you have a really good reason, the Judge is probably going to say, "Sir, I'm going to impute to you, the income that you could be earning. Even if you're not earning it, because I have evidence that leads me to believe you could be earning more money."

The tool of imputation is one that mom is going to use, or ask the state to impute income to you. You have to be aware that if you have a job change and you decide to go from $150,000 a year to $20,000 a year, you better have a darn good PLAUSIBLE reason. Because the judge is going to want to know why you're taking such a huge pay cut.

VOCATIONAL EVALUATION

One of the most useful tools that we have in family court is a vocational evaluation. If mom had a job where she was earning, let's say, $100,000 a year as a mid-level manager at a car dealership, and then decides like, "well, I've had the baby and now I've stayed home for three years and well, there's no jobs out there and I can't get a job", I could ask the court to order mom to go for a vocational evaluation.

When the court orders a vocational evaluation it means that mom is being sent to a career counselor specially trained to determine someone's skills, and who knows the employment marketplace. They are experts who can make a estimate of what someone could or should be earning, based on their prior history, education and work experience.

For example if mom was ordered to an evaluation, she would take some tests on her computer skills, and the evaluator would look at mom's educational background. They would review her resume to see what she's had as previous jobs. Then they'll make a determination as to what, realistically in today's market, mom could be doing to earn money.

A vocational evaluation can be a very powerful tool if it's a highly contested child support case, because mom may find that she may say, "I can't work", but a vocational evaluation may come back and determine, "Well, based on our study and our examination of your skills and your abilities, we see that you actually could be making probably closer to $120,000 a year, because in your marketplace, there's four open jobs for a mid-level manager car dealerships. Why haven't you applied for those?"

Then the court can decide that if she's not going to apply for them, it can certainly say that she could be earning that much money. When a judge imputes that income to her, it can have a huge impact on the child support that dad is ordered to pay.

That's the power of a vocational evaluation, to level the playing field when one party is playing games. It's a very powerful tool that dads need to be aware of, because it can really radically change that child support calculation, and it can also radically change the child custody, because all of a sudden, mom may be more motivated to get a real job.

Fatherhood is loving someone more than your former self.

"Real fatherhood means love and commitment and sacrifice and a willingness to share responsibility and not walking away from one's children."

William Bennett

HOW EXPENSES ARE USED

Let's talk about how expenses are used in child support. It's a big thing that dads have a lot of confusion around and they want to believe that their expenses should count. The reality is this, judges generally don't care about your expenses. They care about what your income is, because the way we calculate child support is your income, mom's income, time that you have the child, those are the big numbers that get used in the calculation.

Dads frequently want to say, "I understand your honor, but I have to be able to pay my car bill, and my phone bill, and my rent, and my utilities. I've got expenses too. I've got to be able to live. If I don't have an apartment, I can't see my kids."

I hate to tell you, but the truth of the matter is this, the law doesn't really care. (Remember who wrote the laws! Mostly lobbyists who are paid for by the beneficiaries of the laws – guess who that is.) The judges who have to enforce the law are concerned with how much money do you have, based on your income. What do you have available to pay mom for child support.

The reason why we have the expenses listed on the income and expense declaration, in California we call it form FL 150, is to use that expense number if dad doesn't show income. Think about this situation, dad goes into court and says, "Well, I'm not working right now and I don't have any money."

The court will ask of dad, "Okay, well, let's take a look at what you put on your FL-150. Your income and expense declaration shows you've got rent of $1,500. Your car payment is $500. Your cell phone payment is $200. That's $2,200. Your food expenses are $400 that's $2,600. You're paying on three credit cards. Another $100 a piece. That's another $300. Now we're at $2,900 and your laundry, utilities, gym membership and other expenses are, let's say, $3,600 a month. Judge is going to ask you, "Sir, I understand you're not working."

"Yes, Your Honor, I'm not working."

"Sir you're telling me you have $3,600 each month in expenses."

"Yes, that's right, Your Honor."

"Okay, is your rent paid?"

"Yes."

"Is your car paid?"

"Yes."

"Is your cell phone paid?"

"Yes."

"Okay, sir. Well, you are telling me that you have no income, but you're also telling me that all of your bills are paid. So how are your bills being paid? I'm going to assume, as the judge, I'm going to assume that if your bills are paid, whether you are showing income or not, you have that amount of income coming in. So I'm going to use that number to calculate your child support."

And this is where dads get tripped up, because they'll put a bunch of numbers in that expenses, they'll increase their expenses, and they'll think they're going to get away with it. And the truth matter is, they're really doing is setting themselves up for failure. That's the number that a judge will use for your income.

If your bills are being paid, obviously that money's coming from somewhere and the judge is going to assume that you've got that money available to pay child support. Remember the judge wants to make sure that that kid is taken care of. If mom ends up on welfare, food stamps, Section Eight, housing, it's costing the state money, and they're going to come after you to repay it, unless you've been paying your child support.

Dads need to be really careful and understand that his expenses are not necessarily anything the judge is going to care about at least until you're not showing any income.

A father's greatest gift is making his child feel unreasonably loved.

> *"You don't raise heroes, you raise sons. And if you treat them like sons, they'll turn out to be heroes, even if it's just in your own eyes."*
>
> **Walter M. Schirra, Sr.**

ABOUT YOUR JOB'S "PERKS"?

When a person receives benefits from their employer, like a free car, or gets to live rent free in an apartment building for being 'the manager' – these are called perquisites, "perks" for short. These benefits may not be taxed at the federal level or state level, they may be considered a "loan" to avoid income taxes, but in family law they are called income.

For the dads who are self-employed, that have their own company, often they're running their life expenses through the business. Things like a gym membership, a car payment, a country club membership, maybe it's a golf membership, these are all perks. Many small business owners may use the company card to pay for groceries. They may be having the cell phone paid for by the business.

TAX DEDUCTIONS

This gets confusing for a lot of people because those can be valid expenses for the IRS. Those could be valid tax deductions. And the IRS says you can legally write off your car, write off some of your meals, write off your employee compensation for your gym membership, your health club membership, your country club membership, all of those are completely valid for the IRS.

But in family law, the court (and your ex's aggressive attorney!) will look at those expenses and say, "well, that's a life expense, and that life expense is actually additional income that should be available to help support the child."

What the court's going to do is, they're going to take those expenses that are valid for the IRS, and pull them out of your tax returns deductions, and put them back into the category of your income. If you've got $100 a month being paid by the company for your phone, that's a deduction for the IRS. The government will allow you to deduct that from income, but Family Court will say, "Wait, wait, wait, wait, bring that over here to income. You've got that expense that's being paid for by the company, that's actually income. You're artificially decreasing your income by calling it a deduction. But we want to bring that back, because somebody had to earn that $100 to pay for your cell phone, and we're going to include that in your income. And we're going to do that with your health club membership. We're going to do that with your country club membership. We're going to do that with your golf membership. We're going to do that with meals. If you're going out to eat it every day, you buy meals for you and your crew that can come back in."

Those totally legal and accepted expenses for Federal tax purposes are perquisites of you owning your own company, those are valid tax deductions. They're also valid in family court as your income.

This is another place where men get bothered, because they don't think it's fair. They think that if the IRS says is a deduction, it should stay a deduction. But in family court, the judge is looking at maximizing the support available for the child.

And so that's what happens when a court looks at your tax returns, and sees a lot of your life expenses are being taken care of by the business. Those expenses are going to be added back into your personal income.

Fatherhood means your heart walks outside your body for the rest of your life.

"Anyone who tells you fatherhood is the greatest thing that can happen to you, they are understating it."

Mike Myers

STRATEGIES FOR FATHERS

Most dads are looking to be fair in their child support. Dads want to pay their fair share of child's expenses, but they also want to have their fair share of child time, and in order to do that frequently, what happens is dads these days have to go into court and get a court order to give them more custodial time, more parenting time with their kids. And it's important for dads to step up and go into court and say, "Your Honor, I am able. I am capable. I've got a flexible work schedule. I live close enough to mom, I live close enough to the school. I want to have more time with my child, because support is not just financial, Your Honor, it's also emotional, it's also educational. I need to have an opportunity to change my child's life by having an active and engaged role in it. They deserve it. It's in their best interest to have a definite relationship with their father, and I'm willing to change my work schedule. I'm willing to change where I live so that I can be more available

You need to be ready to argue to the court that you should have more time, and mom can get a job. I cover that in greater detail in the companion book and video course, DAD's Child Custody Action Plan which is available for you at www.DadsLawSchool.com.

and capable and ready to be there for my child. I've done parenting classes, I've done co-parenting classes, I've done First Aid classes. I've done CPR classes. I am ready. Your Honor, my apartment has been baby proofed. I've got pictures that I've shown you. I've shown pictures to Mom of where I'm living, how I'm living. There's no reason why I shouldn't be an active and engaged father, and when I'm asking for a schedule that's going to allow the child to have equal time with both parents. You, Your Honor, should be granting that."

If you want to learn more about how we do that, I'd invite you to take a look at DAD's Child Custody Action Plan at www.dadslawschool.com. We have both the book and a video course that teaches dads how to really argue to the court, how to get more time with their kids, how to make those arguments about why they're an active and engaged father, how to show to the court that you're an active and engaged father, and all of the reasons why you should have time with your child.

The one thing that's really important is for you to document all of your time. It's important when you're going into court and you're arguing to the judge that you want to modify your child support, and you want to modify your child custody, that you go in with a lot of proof.

You need to remember, moms plot, they plan, they prepare, and then they prove. That's how they're so successful in family court. When you're going into court as a man, you need to be able to plan out your line of attack, prove your arguments, and then be able to get a judge to see that as an active, engaged father, you deserve, and your child deserves, more time with dad.

DAD'S DIARY

The way in which we do that is we document, document, document, document, and it starts with something as simple as going and getting one of those desk calendars from the Office Depot or the staples your office supply store, and literally just marking on it the days that you have your child, when you pick them up, when you drop them off, what did you do with them? And if you spent money, have those receipts available. What I tell dads is, take those receipts, staple them to it. We call it dad's diary, because it's a diary of what have you actually done with your kid?

From my experience of 2 decades in court, mom's planning on coming to court and she'll say something along the lines of this: "He doesn't use the time he's allotted. He's never around. He's a negligent parent. He doesn't know what he's doing. He doesn't know anything about the kid. He doesn't know their best friend, he doesn't know their food allergies, he doesn't know their shoe size."

Dads need to be able to go into court and say "Your Honor. She can say all that, but here's my calendar showing all the time I've spent with my kid. Here's what I know about my kid. I know their best friend is Bobby. I know their shoe size is three. I know this, I know this, I know this."

The reason all of this is important is, when you're going into court, it's going to impact your credibility. You need to be able to show to the judge that you are a credible, capable parent, because mom's going to come in and say, "He's not credible, and he's not capable."

She wants to do what will max out her custody time, because it's how she maxes her child support. You want to make sure that it's fair, and you need to be able to argue to the judge.

DOCUMENTS EQUAL CREDIBILITY

You gain credibility with proof, and that means documents. Same thing with child expenses. This goes for whether it's Boy Scouts, Girl Scouts, soccer practice, medical expenses, school expenses, school supplies, all of those things that are extras above and beyond child support, you should be documenting and keeping track of, so the mom can contribute her fair share.

One of the solutions that I suggest, and I'm a big fan of, is Our Family Wizard. Our Family Wizard is used to communicate between mom and dad. Usually it's email, and it's important with email, because it's archived. Once the email is sent, it can't be changed.

Assume you send mom an email, you can't go in and change what it actually says. So if you put nasty words in there, those words are going to stay forever. And why that's important, it's going to get used in court, because messages from Our Family Wizard are court admissible. Judges know, like and trust Our Family Wizard, they know the value of it, and they rely on it. You can learn more at www.ourfamilywizard.com

Our Family Wizard also has a great tool for tracking expenses. If you go to the doctor's office and you have a $25 copay, you can take that receipt, take a picture, upload it to Our Family Wizard, and now it's going to track that expense.

This makes it simple to see if Dad paid a $25 co-pay. Mom now owes half of that, which is $12.50 mom can then pay that $12.50 through Our Family Wizard, and it's tracked. It now knows that she's paid. You know that you were paid. There's no argument and that goes for you, too.

Mom goes to the dentist, pays a $50 copay, puts it in the system. There's all of a sudden to charge for you $25 copay for the dentist. You pay that with PayPal, or however, Our Family Wizard has you pay. And the reality is that now mom can't go into court and say he owes me all this money for all these co pays, these medical bills and these extracurriculars, no, no, no, no, no, you've gone in and you've got all those records from Our Family Wizard, which, again, are admissible in court to show that you have paid everything you're supposed to pay.

Document, document, document. It's the biggest thing dads need to learn about dealing with child support is document, document, document.

A father's legacy lives in the small kindnesses his children repeat without thinking.

> "The nature of impending fatherhood is that you are doing something that you're unqualified to do, and then you become qualified while doing it."
> **John Green**

MODIFYING CHILD SUPPORT

It's been a while since your last child support hearing and you want to go in to modify your child support award. If you had a change in your pay stub it may be worth it.

Here's what is important to remember, unless there's been a pretty big change in your annual pay and I mean, like 10% or more, probably not worth your time to go in and try and modify your child support.

Generally in California, and most other states, if the change is less than 10%, (or just a temporary break in employment) there's likely no change of circumstances large enough for a court to make a change in child support. So the reality is, if your child support is not going to change a lot, it's probably not worth it for you to draft the paperwork, file it with the court, take off half a day from work, go and argue to the judge as to why your child support should go down.

Mom, similarly, is going to have to be able to argue to the judge that she should get more child support because your income has gone up. This is where she's going to claim, "He's got a second job, he's earning a lot more now, you've got a salary increase, and you're driving a new car. So clearly, you're making more money." She has to prove all those allegations that you're earning a lot more money in order to make that change, and usually it's got to be more than 10% of what your annual income is to change it.

JOB LOSS

Now let's look at what happens when you lose a job. Dads often say, "I need to go into court and change my child support because I no longer have a job." Okay, hold on there, Cowboy. The judge is going to look at that and say, "Well, how likely is it you're going to be out of work for a long period of time, like six months or more." The reality is if you work a job in an industry where it's normal for you to be out of work for a while, or it's easy for you to get hired by a new company, a job loss is going to be considered temporary by the court.

The court's view is that you're probably going to get another job quickly. You'll probably be earning about the same amount of money. So the reality is, courts don't want to change anything.

Even if you go into court and you say, "I lost my job, I want to modify my child support," judges are probably going to look at you and be like, "Hmm, let's wait. Let's see how long you're unemployed."

The problem with waiting is you're still being charged for that child support, and if you're not paying it, you're going to be creating arrearages. You're creating a debt that's will catch up with you sooner or later.

Now the reason why you lost that job is crucial to your arguments. Did you lose that job because the company went out of business? Okay, that's a big factor. The court may look at that and say it's more likely that you're going to have a hard time getting another job.

LAYOFFS

But did you just get laid off temporarily? Is it a seasonal layoff? The court's not going to look at that as a reason to modify child support. You knew it was coming. The court may say, "We're going to analyze that as a part of your child support. We're going to take a look at what's the real income you're earning, and how likely is it that you're going to get rehired?"

Some companies lay off in November, rehire in January. You're only going to be out of work for two months. Most judges won't be willing to change the order for two months.

VOLUNTARY TERMINATION

Did you quit? If you just quit your job That doesn't count. You can't quit your job and say, "I'm not working. I don't have to pay child support". Judges will look at you and say, "We can't make you work. We have that 13th Amendment to the US Constitution thing, but I can say you're going to continue to pay your child support because you voluntarily quit. If you voluntarily quit, that's not grounds to modify your child support".

RETIREMENT

Did you retire because you've reached a certain age and now you want to retire? Well again, the court can look at it and say, we can't make you go ahead and work. What we can do is say, based on what you were earning, what you could be earning, and what your retirement income is, we can base child support on that.

A huge factor in this is whether or not the retirement is done in "Good Faith". So long as you have retired in Good Faith, based on your age, or your physical health, the court will consider that to be a reasonable change in circumstances.

However, if you are NOT doing it in "Good Faith", the court can, and likely will, just impute your regular earning capacity as your income.

WAS IT INVOLUNTARY?

Did you get fired? People think "I got fired from my job. I don't have a job. I can't pay my child support". No, because the court's going to look at that and say, "Well, what did you do to get fired? Did you violate a company policy? Did you fail a drug test? Did you do some affirmative action like sexually harass somebody that caused you to get fired? Were you rude to a customer that caused you to get fired?"

All of those are reasons that the court's will look at and decide, "It was your behavior that caused you to get fired. Had you acted properly, you would still have that job. You would still have that income. We're not going to let you off the hook because you acted poorly and now say you can't pay your child support".

The court will impute the income to you, because you could be working, but for your own bad actions. You need to remember that a court will look at several layers of what happened to figure out, should you pay, and can you actually pay your child support? Which is where they are leaning.

Being a father is planting trees you may never sit under.

> *"There's so much negative imagery of black fatherhood. I've got tons of friends that are doing the right thing by their kids, and doing the right thing as a father - and how come that's not as newsworthy?"*
>
> **Will Smith**

HANDLING CHILD SUPPORT OWED - ARREARAGES

CALCULATING INTEREST DUE

When someone gets behind in paying their child support, the state imposes an annual interest rate. Now in California, that interest rate is 10%. What that means is, if you owe a $500 a month child support, you're going to pay $50 as an annual interest charge for that $500 and it's going to be charged each month. I don't mean $50 per month, but $50 over the course of the year. So that $500 payment is getting charged $4 for the first month, $4 for the next month, $4 for the next month, so that over the course of the year, it's going to be a total of $50 but now that $500 child support payment is now $550. That means that each year that you're past due on a single payment, you owe $550.

EXAMPLE OF INTEREST OF CHILD SUPPORT OWED

Child Support Due	Annual Interest Rate	Annual Interest charge	Monthly Interest Charge
$500	10%	$50.00	$4.17

HOW CHILD SUPPORT PAYMENTS ARE APPLIED

There is a family code section that explains how any payments you make are applied. When you make a payment today, it will be applied to the Child Support due for this month, any extra amount you pay will be applied to any INTEREST that you owe for prior months, and FINALLY, any money left over will be applied to the actual past due child support.

That's how people get really far behind, really quickly on their child support. Because the payments go to the current payment due, then the past due interest, and THEN to what you actually owed for child support. You can see how a very deep financial hole gets dug, in very little time, and it's super hard to dig yourself out of it.

If you start getting behind, you have to get caught up as quickly as possible. Because you have payments that will continue to add interest. If all you're paying is the old interest, while you're still adding new interest, even though the debt may be a year old, and you may have paid a ton of money towards it, it doesn't actually get to the actual child support payment until all the interest charges are paid.

Under **California Family Code §695.221,** *payments toward child support arrears are applied in this order:*

1. **First, to current child support due** *for that month (if any);*

2. **Then, to any accrued interest** *on past-due support;*

3. **Finally, to the principal** *amount of the past-due support.*

ENFORCEMENT BY THE STATE

The fast rate at which back support and interest grows is why you want to stay on top of the payments, and not get behind in your child support.

In California (and most states) the DMV can suspend your driver's license once you're behind on your child support payments. That's a problem for most people, because if you can't drive, you can't get to work, and if you can't get to work, you can't earn the money to pay back the child support that you're behind on. It's kind of crazy the way that works.

There's a solution to that, though, if you're behind in your child support, you go into court and ask the judge to release your driver's license and put you on a payment plan. Those work and so long as you're making a small payment on what's owed every month your driver's license will still be valid.

There are new laws in California that are relaxing the harsh impacts of Driver's License suspension. People who were behind on their support and having their licenses suspended, had to spend time and money going to court to get their licenses released – which happened often – so it wasn't all that effective a tool for the state. It was also punishing the poorest of people who were paying the least amount of support, and making life even harder for them.

This is crucial for dads who've gotten behind, because as soon as you get behind and they suspend your driver's license, if you get pulled over, then the state can impound your car because you're driving without a license. Now you've got to pay to get your car back from impound at $100 to $200 a day while you still owe all that back child support. Now, you can't get to work because you don't have your driver's license.

The cascading effect of problems all stem from getting behind in child support by a month or two, can lead to losing your job, losing your car, losing your ability to get to work if you're jailed, and that's when life becomes really crazy for a lot of people.

That's why it's important to stay on top of this stuff. Now, what I mean by staying on top of this is if you're making payments, you need to make sure that those payments get recorded as child support.

MOM OWED CHILD SUPPORT

If you just give your child's mother cash, what's going to happen is this: she will deny that you actually paid it, and you don't have any proof that you paid it. Which means you STILL OWE IT, and will have to pay it again.

That's why I advise that you pay by check, wire transfer, Zelle, CashApp, PayPal, Venmo, or money order. You should only use a payment method that allows you to mark it as child support. Every payment you make should have a date and what month the support is for. When you pay the March 2025 child support it should be marked on the memo or some place so that when you have to go back into court, you can say to a judge, "She said I didn't pay it. But here's the proof, Your Honor, that I did pay March of 2025."

It's very important, because if there's an argument over whether or not that month is paid, if you don't have the proof, and they say it wasn't paid, you're going to owe it.

Plus, you're going to owe interest on it, and that's going to become a much bigger problem going forward, when you have arrearages.

If it's just money that's owed to your child's mom, sometimes you can negotiate that overdue past due child support. Maybe mom's willing to make a deal with you. Sometimes I've had a mom say, "Alright, just give me half, and we'll call it even. The kids are 18. We're done. I don't want anything more from you. I want to move on with my life." It's not often but it can happen with moms where you can negotiate a payoff of the arrearage.

STATE OWED MONEY

However, if that money you owe to the ex has been assigned to the state, because mom was collecting welfare or food stamps, the state will not ever, under any circumstances, waive the money that is owed. You're going to owe that forever, which is one of the reasons why you have to make sure that you're staying on top of your child support.

Because so long as you're paying what you've been court ordered to pay, the state won't come back at you for more money, but you have to be current with that, the state will never forgive money that was paid for food stamps, medical, any government funds that were paid to support a child when you had an obligation to support that child and didn't. The state's going to come after you.

Sometimes people are worried that the judge is going to put them in jail if they owe child support. Can they? Yes. Do they do it often? No.

Honestly, here's my experience. In 27 years of practicing Family Law (limited to California though), I've only seen one person get put in jail for not paying their child support in California.

Jail is a last resort for the court, because they have other tools like license suspension, passport denial, wage garnishments, property liens and reporting to the credit agencies that are preferred ways to put pressure on someone to pay their child support.

What generally happens is the court tries to put pressure on you by taking your driver's license, taking your passport, taking your professional license, like your general contractor's license, your barber license, your real estate license. If you're a lawyer, your bar license can be suspended. All of those are ways in which the state can put pressure on you without having you go to jail.

The one time I saw somebody go to jail, the person owed over $100,000 in child support and walked into court dripping in gold, wearing brand new Jordans, lots of flashy clothes. And the judge said, "Why aren't you paying your child support?" And the man replied, "Because I can't." The judge looked at him and said, "I don't believe you." And then the other side came out with bank statements that showed he actually had enough money in the bank and he just wasn't paying it. That's when a judge said, "Okay, you're going to jail, and you can get out of jail as soon as you pay your past due child support." Unsurprisingly, that's what ended up happening.

That's literally what it takes, you've got to be in the situation where you have the money in the bank and you're just refusing to pay it. That's when a judge will put you in jail. In general if you're just behind on your child support, you're probably not going to go to jail unless there's another reason. In the above case, the guy was actually in contempt of court. He met ALL FOUR of the factors for a contempt because he was 1) ordered to pay it, 2) had the ability to pay it, 3) he wasn't paying it, and it was a 4) willful refusal to pay.

The ability to pay is a big factor, because if you don't have the ability to pay, the court can't enforce the order. You have to be able to comply with a court order. If you can't comply with a court order, like you physically don't have the money in your account to write the check, the court can't make you do something that you can't do.

That's why, if you're going to get in trouble with the court, you're most likely going to get in trouble with the court by being in contempt when you have the ability to comply, but you refuse to.

So don't do that. It's a bad idea. Other than that, you need to just stay as current as you can with your child support. You need to modify it when you can.

Please understand that there are many things you can do to help yourself. Keeping track of your records, pay her but not in cash. Pay her, in a way that is traceable. Have the memo field marked with the specific month that is being paid for, and have a record so that when you have to go into court to defend yourself, you've got the evidence and you have the proof.

*A father who listens raises
children who speak.*

"Fatherhood is the best thing that could happen to me, and I'm just glad I can share my voice."

Dwayne Wade

ENFORCEMENT

Enforcement. This is the way the government's going to enforce their government order for you to pay child support. Number one, it's going to be a wage garnishment.

WAGE GARNISHMENT

Now, if you have a regular job, the court can make an order that the child support you have to pay can come directly from your employer. They take it right out of your paycheck.

A lot of men don't like this. A lot of guys think that it makes them look like a deadbeat or a loser or a scumbag. They say, "I can pay my child support." I understand that there's an ego part of you that says I shouldn't have the money just taken from me.

Here's the thing, the employers don't really care. They don't really look at you differently because you have a wage garnishment. It happens a lot. From my perspective as a lawyer, it's actually kind of a good thing. Because now there is a third party involved.

There is this government agency that's keeping track of the payments. They're keeping track of the money taken from your paycheck, and they're supposed to be giving it to mom. It's out of your hands. Now it's on them. If they screw up, it's their responsibility to explain to mom why she hasn't gotten her money.

This can be a really, useful thing for you. Because it's one less thing to worry about. You get your paycheck, and that's what you get to live on. You know what your dollar amount is and you're not going to get behind. And not getting behind is crucial to not screwing up your life, because if you get behind now you've got enforcement issues.

Now they can suspend your driver's license, and they can take your passport. The state can suspend your professional license. If you're a general contractor, a real estate agent, a barber, a plumber, electrician, whatever you do that has a state agency involved that authorizes you to work that can get suspended if you get behind in your child support.

In the long run, a wage garnishment can be one of your best friends, because if you get behind now, you can ask for an audit, and an audit will have them actually produce all of the documents, all of the money they've taken from you, which they may screw up on, but you have your pay stubs, and all of your pay stubs are going to have that line item of wage garnishment for child support. So now you've got your proof that they screwed up. It's on them to fix it with mom.

BANK LEVIES

The other big tool for enforcement actions happen are bank levies. If you get behind in your child support, the state will come to collect child support, can and will just go right into your bank account, take the money from you. They will just take that money if there's money sitting in a bank account, apply it towards your past due child support and eventually give it to mom.

TAX REFUNDS

The other thing that can happen with enforcement is this; if you are due a tax refund for a year, that tax refund, whether it's from the state or the feds, can be intercepted. That means they will take your tax refund that was supposed to go to you, and they will give it to mom as payment towards the child support. It's not a great solution. I don't recommend you get behind in your child support. You should stay on top of your support so that you're going to get your tax refund, and so that your bank account won't get levied.

Those are the two big ways in which the state will get their money for the child support. You need to be aware that those are possibilities, and how to fight them. The best way is don't get behind in your child support.

Fatherhood is the slow surrender of sovereignty.

"What I love most about fatherhood is the opportunity to be a part of the development process of a new life."

Seal

MOVING FORWARD

Hopefully you've learned a lot from this book. I just want to wrap up with a few things to remind you, going forward, it's not a life sentence. Child support is something that can be devastating for a moment, but it does end eventually, and so long as you keep working, you can get out from under it.

You can get it all paid off, and move on with your life, as long as you stay current on your child support. Usually, those kids, when they age out at 18, sometimes 19, if they're still in high school, will age out. Once they age out the court order expires and as a consequence, your obligations to your ex will end.

Once a child has aged out, and child support ends, if there are arrears, if there is money owed, you'll have to keep paying until that's paid off. Remember, it's still going to be collecting interest, and sometimes the state will actually put penalties on top of that interest, but that's pretty rare.

Keep detailed records, keep those bank statements, keep those paystubs, because you want to be able to prove, until you're absolutely done, that you've been paying your child support. You want to be able to show that each and every payment has been made, and be able to prove it to the court if you have to.

I always recommend that you get a "Closing Order" that states you have paid all your support and that the case is "CLOSED".

If you've got further questions, feel free to reach out to me. It's david@dadslawschool.com

And remember, I think you're fucking awesome.

The best fathers raise children who don't need them, but still want them.